A Ribbon of Gray Patched in Gold

Linda Robinson

PHEW PUBLISHING

www.PHEWpublishing.com
Hardcover: 979-8-9916991-2-9
Paperback: 979-8-9916991-1-2
Kindle: 979-8-9916991-3-6

Production by Concierge Marketing Inc., www.conciergemarketing.com

Printed in the United States of America
10 9 8 7 6 5 4 3 2 1

To my family, my loved ones, and my Higher Power.

Contents

Poems

Thoughts Seeking A Melody

Short Stories

Poems

What Matters

It matters not, the clouds, the clear
What matters is, that you are here
Another day to feel, explore
To walk through that new opened door
To grasp at hope, to touch a hand
And write new lines upon the sand
Say one kind word, forget the bad
Be thankful for the love you've had
What matters is, how to forgive
To live in peace, peacefully live

December 2010

Peace & Rain

Peace and rain, I pray for these

War and drought, I pray for ease

Peace and rain upon our land

Simple things, a healing hand

Peace and rain upon our earth

Bring relief and bring rebirth

Peace and rain and fond desire

Quench a flame and numb a fire

The world to grow in healthy gain

I pray for peace, I pray for rain

Date unknown

Just Sometimes

Sometimes you have to let things go

Let things go to let them grow

Be sad but bold and say goodbye

Let life unfold with one last cry

And though that love did disappear

It may come back another year

Somewhere beyond that time of grief

You found a way to feel relief

Sometimes things happen for the best

And broken hearts are laid to rest

Then someday soon, time will release

Two hearts renewed, two hearts at peace

December 5, 2010

Cat

I need to take a walk but I'd rather take a nap

A recliner and a nap with a cat on my lap

Take advantage of the sun with the warmth and the heat

The recliner and the heat with the cat on my feet

Feel the warmth all around, the recliner is the place

With a nap and the heat and the cat by my face

2021

Dumb Old Cat

He opens the door to my bedroom

To signal it's time to get up

He tells me get busy, I'm hungry

If I've been gone for a while, he sits close by

Guarding me after my return

He has to drink out of my ice water

Flips around my foot, bites my arm

Naps on newly folded clothes

Soft as satin, eyes all knowing

Smarter than my sister's

Dumb old one-eyed dog

I haven't convinced her of that yet

Dumb old cat

2010

Third Cat Thought

Never met a cat I didn't like

Reach out my hand, it gives me a strike

Say hello, it gives me a growl

Move away, it shows me a scowl

They don't trust, I get it

But I just wanted to pet it

January 1, 2024

I LOVE YOU

25 years

How fast can 25 years go?
I guess I can say I don't care or don't know.
But I know that it's long enough to get children raised,
to weather life storms and to come out unfazed.
To have felt all the feelings this world presents
and arise from the rubble with most of my sense.
To know that pure joy is like liquid gold
as it seeps through your fingers just too hard to hold.
To know seconds and minutes snowball into years,
picking up laughter and sadness and tears.
Like a breeze and a blink or a breath and a sigh,
every day was a year that turned into goodbye.
But to know every sunrise and set was a blessing,
like God reached down and I felt his caressing.
More precious than silver were these years spent.
I just wish I knew where all the time went.
Every day I would wait for the future to start
while I tucked every memory deep in my heart.
Like a butterfly born to flutter away,
25 years was just part of today.

2005

When My Girls Were Little

When my girls were little
Seems hair was never brushed
Like flowing, tumbling flowers
Silk ribbons, blown and rushed
When my girls were little
Their hair swept off, aside
In bouncing, fluffed disorder
Revealing smiles wide
Simple play and wonder
Compelling, strong, yet messed
I'd gaze upon their faces
And feel my heart so blessed
Those days spent growing, playing
Running, cheeks aflushed
The breeze, the sun, the moment
Cared not, their hair was brushed

2015

Four in One

One with lovely, pink flushed cheeks
And honey colored hair
One with curls of blond so soft
With energy to spare
One looked different, darker eyes
A blanket by her side
And One with roundness in her face
A smile sweet and wide
One who loved a doll and crib, One who loved a cat
One who loved a crayon book, One loved a ball and bat
One could stop a grounder, One could pitch the ball
One could dawn a catcher's mitt, One could do it all
One is kind and gentle, One is keen and smart
One is strong and steady, One has a golden heart
One has sweet demeanor, One has a thorny edge
One is calm and mild, One flirts around a ledge
One in all, in likeness
Four, in reality
Four lovely pretty roses
God has given me

September 23, 2022

My Mother

I miss my mother like a little child

And she's gone to the grocery store

I look out the window to see lights down the road

Try to hear the kitchen door

I miss her voice and her soft kind eyes that held secrets I never knew

I never thought about her thoughts, she missed her mother too

How could the day come that I would be grown

And not hear the kitchen door

I miss my mother, she's gone away

I'm a little child once more

March 2018

Ten Rules in Life

1. Be a big sister with all good advice
2. When the stove is hot, always say "HICE"
3. A girl can get scraggly, so trim up her tresses
4. And never pass down matching belts with their dresses
5. Love flowers and birds and the land that you farm
6. Enjoy all the grandkids and all of their charm
7. Drink half-heated coffee that's been there awhile
8. Then weep for your losses, remember her smile
9. Find silent time to sit and to pray
10. And say a Rosary every day

September 28, 2022

Scary Things
By The
River

RIVER THAT WAY

C o f e

River Ahead

LANE TO THE
RIVER

Log

The River

A thermos of coffee, a walk down the lane

Let nature surround me and I won't complain

Down by the river to rest on a log

A little more coffee, a scruffy old dog

Birds softly moving, the river goes slow

I'm sitting here calm with my cup of joe

It's easy to worry, the days may be hard

But I've got a river in my backyard

March 9, 2018

October Surprise

Like glint of star through cloudy night

An out of place, untimely sight

These lilacs stood and held their form

And made me feel last summer's warm

A lovely faint, soft purple tint

Although the winter tried to hint

October cool had made some room

For lilac's unexpected bloom

Here, hope and beauty at its best

And filled my soul with quiet rest

October 31, 2012

Butterflies

Running into butterflies
A lifelong love affair
A flower child on the green
With daisies in her hair

A butterfly that floats along
And lands upon her hand
The peace and beauty so profound
We grasp to understand

The girl in twirling floral skirt
Lifts hands toward the sky
With butterfly in palm, she tries
To softly coax it, "Fly"

My running into butterflies
Does take a dreadful twist
My truck and I and windshield
Do wish we could have missed

December 13, 2014

AND EVEN MORE STRANGE THINGS IN THERE

The Fort

If you walk down the alley, you see a great world
Of weeds that are blooming and leaves that are curled
The foxes have made a home 'long the side
And up in the higher, the squirrels try to hide
The barbed wire fence reminds you 'it's' there
And so it might be that Fall's in the air
And who knows what secret an old log does hold
So peel back the moss, let the story unfold
To one side, a canopy, trees and that sort
So thick in the summer, it looks like a fort
At times, you can hear the shouts of the young
With freedom and fancy and joy on their tongue
So much children learn about trees and the birds
Exclaim their delight with hundreds of words

And this was the world with children at play
'Twas a long time ago and a lifetime away
So tonight, I'll sit on the porch on the breeze
I'll listen for shouts from the Fort in the trees

September 20, 2022

Black Bird Barrage

A swirling, evil scourge, descending

Then instantly, a plume, ascending

A silky ribbon floating, going

Then back toward the gold corn, growing

They rise again in such perfection

A million cells in one direction

To dip and dive in noble awe

Twist and turn, defy all law

Every moment, so succinct

Now they are gone, oh no, I blinked

2018

Dandelion Saga

Out of the winter, came the robin
      And its entourage
Out of the cold, grew the weed
      Peaking up near my garage
Out of the gray, came a smile
      Missing for so long
And from the wind, finally softened
      A breeze disguised as song
There, in song, was light and magic
      Tilting up my chin
The sound, I could not find the source
      Perhaps, was from within
With clarity, new light, new breath
      Continue, learn and flow
Accept the concrete with its cracks
      Let dandelions grow

2023

Looking for Angels

How I pray for Angels near
A Sapientia at my ear
A Counselor to guide my day
A Navigator with the way

Ascender lift me from the flame
Absolver pardon human shame
My own Saint Michael hear my call
Rescue me from sin and fall

Author write a happy end
Sculptor shape my knee to bend
Alpha take me through my birth
Omega rise me from this Earth

A pilgrimage to Heaven's Gate
For this I long, I hope, I wait
Sacred peace embrace my soul
Complete my spirit, make me whole

October 18, 2012

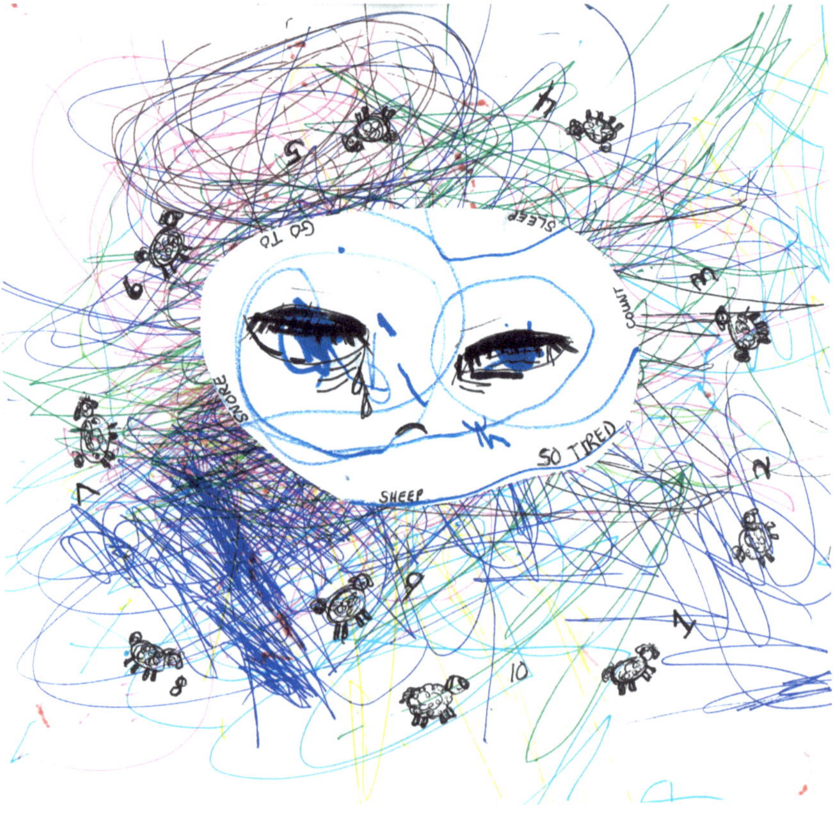
GO TO
SLEEP
COUNT
SHEEP
SO TIRED
SNORE
10

Sleep

Would Mr. Sandman find me soon, I'm here beneath the evening moon

I wish for me a midnight trance, would Morpheus perform his dance

I tried to rock, I tried to read, to close my eyes, did not succeed

The tube from which all colors seep, send mortal men into their sleep

Could not succeed in boring me to close my eyes for reverie

But not to find at least a loll and take my place like sleeping doll

I told my brain to count the sheep, did not the ovine promise keep

I tried to nod and fake closed eyes, but brain saw through my weak disguise

Could nature ever find my drowse, I guess just that, which mind allows

It looks like dreams be absent here, perhaps it's nightmares I fear

And now the clock proceeds to say, the tick of six is on the way

And seven soon to follow on, the break of light, the break of dawn

And now the day is full in sight, I'll try again, perhaps tonight

And if tonight should fail me too, well, I just don't know what to do

Mid-2000

Wyoming Wanderer

Roaming wolf cried out for rest

Tired from its earthly quest

Finally peace the soul took flight

On gentle breeze through starry night

Spirit love like morning mist

Was never caged but did exist

Spirit love now wanders free

And drifts into eternity

March 7, 2016

Good Night

She tells her baby goodnight
Her baby wrapped in light
A kiss upon the face
As lonely arms embrace

The gentle Angel nears
To share the moment's tears
Her wings are crest in gold
She comes to gently hold

The baby sleeps in peace
Will faith in God increase
The stoic Angel keeps
The woman gently weeps

Time cannot stop the yearn
Would God decrease the burn
With hope and faith and prayer
And love that lingers there

Early 2000

Life Went On

When a man in the neighborhood died
The quiet news
Rippled through the early morning hours

People drank coffee and drove off to work
Dogs barked, routines continued
While warm breezes were met with awe
And appreciation for the mild March weather

Children rode their bikes, oblivious
To the sting of loss

And although death suspended reality
For several hours that morning
Life continued to push everything forward that day

Date unknown

Her Stone Read

Her name was something somebody
A woman not well known
She carried lonely feelings
When her children had all grown

Her life was lived quite simply
One day one week one year
She managed her emotions
With a laugh a sigh a tear

Her soul had many secrets
Of dreams and goals she had
But everyday seemed empty
She grew old being sad

And time had left her looking
At things gone unachieved
And she lived disappointed
At what she once believed

The world that did surround her
The spinning time and space
It only made her weary
She couldn't keep the pace

The growing old was hurtful
Her heart could take no more
And at her funeral no one knew
Her death came years before

August 16, 2012

Lillie Miller

The lovely Lillie Miller
Of 1932
She lies beneath the shaded grass
Beneath a pine that grew
She lies in wait day in day out
To hear a friendly voice
She does not smile or say a word
But that is not her choice
I wonder what she looked like
The color she would wear
And if she chose to gently
Tie a ribbon through her hair
And in her youth did Lillie have
The dreams a woman dreams
And now so many years beyond
She's just a ghost it seems
And did she ever speak of love
Or birth and life and death
And did her lover ever whisper
Softly 'neath his breath
The lovely Lillie Miller
She cannot hear me call
I wonder if she calmly waits
Or if she's there at all

Date unknown

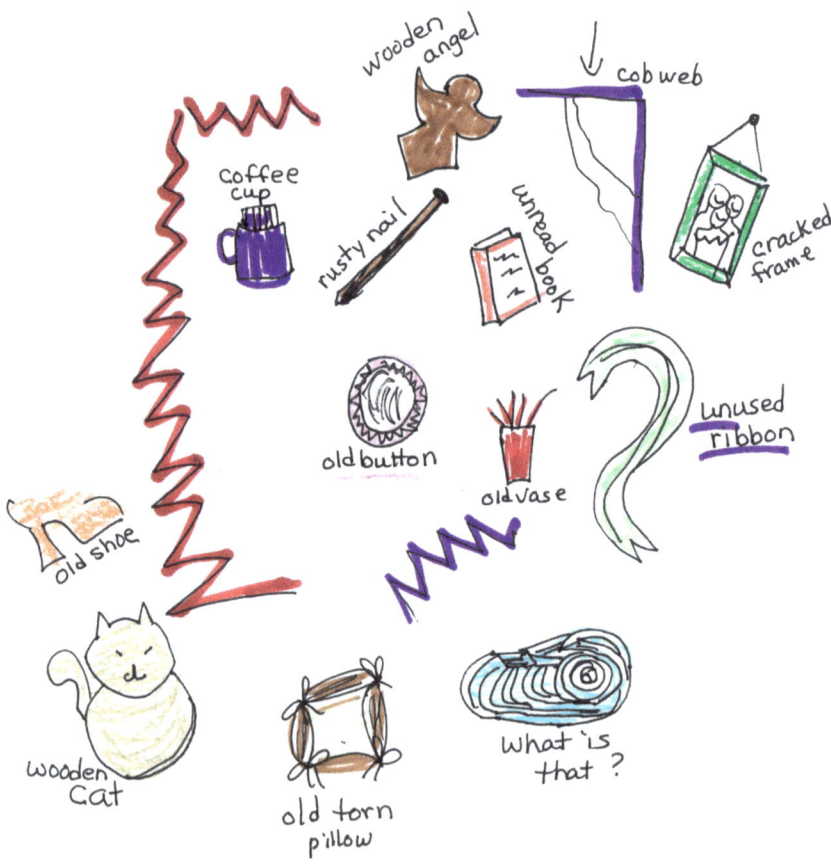

wooden angel

cob web

coffee cup

rusty nail

unread book

cracked frame

old button

old vase

unused ribbon

old shoe

wooden cat

old torn pillow

what is that?

Ashes to Dust

Ashes to ashes

Dust to dust

What is the meaning of all this stuff

Dust to dust

Knicks to knacks

All the little things with cracks

Cracks and hollows

Webs and all

Filling the shelves we hang on walls

Rusty things that I find fun

Will get thrown when I'm done

Yes we folks we love our stuff

Even all the stuff to dust

2023

Brain Block

Yes, I could go on and on
      About the poems I write
Another verse, a few more words
      It's only two at night

And then I think a catchy phrase
      And one more funny verse
But then one word's not fitting
      And I strive to break the curse

Then days go on and months go past
      My brain gets filled with doubt
I don't know how I cannot seem
      To cure this dreadful drought

Date unknown

Re-ing

I'm rethinking my rethinking
and reducing my dunking
with donuts and bonuses
sugar and sweetening!

Sweetening, laughter
and talking of giving
and giving is good
and good is for living!

Living is best done
floating not sinking
So up from your sinking
and start your rethinking!

No rainfulls of painfulls
No painful disdaining
No losses or crosses
So let's start regaining!

Regaining with laughing
with praying and giving
and start with the beautiful
beauty of living!

2021

I Want Some More...

Kisses and hugs, whiskey and jugs

Jokes to laugh at, swings of the bat

Honey from bees, shade from the trees

Matchless snowflakes, more birthday cakes

Trinkets to dust, nails with old rust

Nightmare ends, coffee with friends

Ink to go write, flights from a kite

Mosquitoes quite smashed, lightning that's flashed

Old cats by the lane, more scents of new rain

A little more time for one really good rhyme

Is that too much to ask?

One more tuck from that flask?

(Oh the flask of life)

December 2023

So Now

So now I'll dream of falling stars and sterling cars

Suns of gold and midnight's cold

And fluffy cats I'll wear as hats

And mysteries that don't unfold

And all the secret caves

And the great crashing waves

That pristine castle out of reach

And that plump, pinkish, ripened peach

And all and all the ticking clocks

And lovely purple hollyhocks

That grow as high as high can seem

And my never-ending dream to dream

Date unknown

Climb

I'm gonna climb… to the top of the Hill
I'm gonna climb… to the top of the Hill
I think it's time… go to the top of the Hill
To live my live at the top of the Hill

Don't let me stumble… at the top of the Hill
Don't let me crumble… at the top of the Hill
I take my trouble… to the top of the Hill
Help me be humble at the top of the Hill

I feel the thorns… goin' up to that Hill
I hear the storms… goin' up to that Hill
The blood he poured… goin' up to that Hill
Is my reward at the top of the Hill

I'll see the sun… at the top of the Hill
The battle won… at the top of the Hill
New life begun… at the top of the Hill
Thy will be done at the top of the Hill

There is a place… at the top of the Hill
A shiny face… at the top of the Hill
A loving grace… at the top of the Hill
Time to embrace the top of the Hill

Time to embrace the top of the Hill

Praise Be His

There's a light in the distance
There's a light on the hill
And as I fall into my sinful ways
I know he loves me still

Chorus
Praise to Him, all praise be His
Praise to Him, all praise be His

He's the light of forgiveness
His forgiveness will heal
And as I walk towards His mercy and His ways
I know my heart will fill

With praise to Him, all praise be His
Praise to Him, all praise be His

He is the Father in Heaven
He is the Son on the Cross
And as His Holy Spirit leads us on our way
We are not orphans lost

And so I sing
Praise to Him, all praise be His
Praise to Him, all praise I will give

I will praise Him forever
All my praise I will give
I will remember that light on the hill
He died so I could live

And always my praise to Him, all praise be His
Praise to Him, all praise be His

Perfect Walk

A perfect walk on a perfect day
A perfect breeze to guide my way
It gives me time to think and pray
On a perfect walk on a perfect day
On a perfect walk on a perfect day

A perfect sky above my head
I felt blessed when I crawled out of bed
The world was still but so much was said
On a perfect walk on a perfect day
On a perfect walk on a perfect day

Step by step down the road I go
I don't know a lot but that's what I know
And I know enough to just let it all go
To a perfect God on a perfect day
On a perfect walk on a perfect day

I turned my face to a setting sun
This walk is over but I ain't done
And I'll keep goin' till this race is won
To a perfect place in a perfect way
On a perfect walk on a perfect day

Old Broken Heart

He spent most of his time sit'in at the bar
With a few dollars left to put gas in his car
He had a warm smile that could bum a cigar
But he lives with the scar of an old broken heart
Yeah, he lives with the scar of an old broken heart

He never was one to push around blame
He seemed content to watch the old football game
But after she left, life just wasn't the same
And he lives with the pain of an old broken heart
Yeah, he lives with the pain of an old broken heart

And the kids come around every now and again
And he tries to remember how lucky he's been
But after she left he lost his best friend
And the pain never ends with an old broken heart
Yeah, the pain never ends with an old broken heart

Now he's sit'in at the table and his coffee's growin' cold
And the pain in his shoulder tells him he's growin' old
And he wonders whatever happened to *to have and to hold*
Yeah, life's pretty cold with an old broken heart
Yeah, life's pretty cold with an old broken heart

Life's cruel and cold with an old broken heart
And it's hard growing old with an old broken heart.

Short Stories

The Nativity Cat

This story began way before I got there.
I was out finding scraps in the cold night air.
I was pawing around the warm Inn's light.
The owner had thrown out old bread from the night.

But I felt a chill, it was time to go home.
I looked forward to reaching my warm, safe dome.
So quickly, I headed away from footfall,
To the town's dim edge with no people at all.

I crept high through a pasture and up over snow.
That's when I noticed an odd nighttime glow.
That glow made me crouch, unsure of its power.
But soon, it lent warmth in that very dark hour.

That glow lit my path, like a Heavenly Beam.
An Angelic star led me home, it would seem.
Still, I kept my eyes keen, and I kept my eyes cast,
Till I reached that old stable, my sanctum, at last.

As soon as I entered, I felt the warm air.
And the stable was filled with love and care.
But something was odd in that lowly retreat.
There, livestock mulled softly, with moo, neigh, and bleat.

The animals paced and were stirring, yet calm.
As they kept the barn warm with their breath and their balm.
Still, it seemed there was motion, excitement and din.
And it looked like some humans had stopped to come in.

Like a shadowy figure, I crept like a ghost,
Over mound, over bundle, and then bale and post.
And I wondered, my curious nature came out.
What were the livestock excited about?

Then I rested, concealed, but high up like a crow
To take in the scene going on down below.
It wasn't a fight or a fray or a stranger,
But humans, quite meek, huddled next to a manger.

A woman and man I was looking upon
And I wasn't afraid, all anxiety was gone.
A whisper of peace floated down overall
And there in the center lie something quite small.

Could it be that I saw with my very sharp eyes?
A newborn, a baby! Oh what a surprise!
Now my hearing is faded, my ears, a bit cracked,
But my natural instinct is still quite intact.

My paws felt a tremble, my whiskers had tensed.
This birth was life changing for all men, I sensed.
This thing that had happened was much more than special.
It was Heaven on Earth, sublime and celestial.

And right at that time, my fur bristled and shook
And I had to climb down for a much closer look.
I began my descent to the straw-covered floor.
But alas, three more people came through the old door.

I hid myself down, not sure what to expect.
But I could now tell they were posing no threat.
They knelt down on knee as if to revere,
And the sweetness of Angelic song touched my ear.

They all crowded 'round as close as they could,
And the strangers brought presents and things that seemed good.
Like some things called frankincense, gold, and myrrh,
But I thought, is there not a blanket of fur?

Why even small kittens once born in this barn,
Were covered with something called fabric and yarn.
Now the straw and the hay provided some heat,
But I wished for more cover for small hands and feet.

Perhaps I could help, I spoke in a trill.
I could hover quite closely to take off the chill.
So I stepped very close and crouched again, low.
Just to see how near to the Babe I could go.

I felt safe, I felt sure, as closer I walked.
And could hear a low voice, as the woman, she talked.
Then all of a sudden the tuft on my head,
Was touched very softly and the young woman said.

Hello dear old kitty. How lovely a face.
You must know we're thankful for use of your space.
And please tell your friends we're grateful that they,
Allowed us to use their warmth and their hay.

Then she patted my head so gently and light.
And that was the moment pure peace filled the night.
A peace worth more all the jewels on the Earth,
Like the scene I witnessed with this Holy Birth.

And so the time passed and I'm not sure how much.
But I loved her caress and her every touch.
To never be kicked at, or hit, or be shoved,
A cat's only wish is a wish to be loved.

Now the humans were talking in tones very low,
Of travel and planning, and which way to go.
I had hoped they could stay to live with us here,
But I knew their departure was imminent, near.

I'll never forget all the kindness they showed.
And sadly I watched as they took to the road.
My heart was in woe as they left on that day.
But somehow I knew that love led their way.

I believed in their journey so filled with great Grace.
I believed in their love for the whole human race.
They offered their love to such simple a lair.
And we will recall the Babe who slept there.

In the midst of God's creatures, they stayed to share joy,
The Wise Men, the Parents, the loved Little Boy.
In that time, I had glee, I had bliss, all of that,
And a Family who loved a scruffy old cat.

The Trade

Once there was a battered world all blanketed in gray
And people wailed and hid their eyes; they could not face the day

The world was stripped of love and hope, all torn by hate and war
The poor, lost souls, consumed by fear, had wanted so much more

But in the darkness, in the din, was one soul, weak and old
A woman who had no great gift, no silver, silk or gold

And yet she wished to ease the pain, to bring the world some aid
But all she knew was how to cry, for she was so afraid

So simply, she began to weep, to cry for all the world
And in her tears were just one hope, that all her cries be heard

She cried for all the little babes aborted in the womb,
For all the unloved helpless ones whose lives were filled with doom

She wept for children left behind, abandoned just for drugs.
She cried for teens who never feel the warmth of loving hugs

She wept for all the broken hearts, for those who lived in pain
For those who never see the sun, but only feel the rain

She cried for wars and soldiers who return in body bags
She cried for countries bombed and torn, their people clothed in rags

She cried for lonely widows who wonder about death
And cried for those with illness, awaiting their last breath

Yet all the tears that left her eyes could never ease the sorrow
Would never help the world to heal or make a bright tomorrow

And so she stopped and dried her eyes, she wiped her tears away
And she began a brand new plan, yes, she began to pray

She prayed for all the families, for husbands and for wives
And for the world to live in hope, for all the precious lives

She prayed for strength and courage and she prayed for peaceful things
For God to send His touches down on Golden Angel Wings

And then she thought, if one small prayer, sincere and from the heart
Can change one man, one simple man, then isn't that a start

And over time, one prayer can grow to change the human race
Then hearts and minds can join to make the World a better place

Early 2000

Oh the Possibilities

I wanted to be an actor but I didn't have the face
Wanted to be an astronaut but was too scared of space
Thought about being a singer couldn't carry a tune
Wanted to get a full time job but I couldn't get up by noon
Wanted to be a model but I didn't have the poise
Wanted to raise some children but I couldn't stand the noise
Wanted to be a dancer but I couldn't cut a rug
Could've been a bar maid but I always broke the mug
Could've been a politician didn't like giving speeches
Should've been a fisherman didn't like touching leeches
Could've been a chef didn't like doing dishes
Wanted to be a genie had no wand or wishes
Could've been a nun just too lazy to pray
Should've been a quarterback but always forgot the play
Thought about being a cowboy couldn't ride a horse
Maybe be a Viking but never was a Norse
Thought about working in a zoo couldn't stand animal hair
Maybe work in an apple orchard rather have a pear
Coulda woulda shoulda nothing more to say
Never climbed a mountain couldn't find the way

2006

And so,

it is...

A Ribbon Patched in Gold

Years ago, I had a dream
God was giving out prizes
His bag was full of modest things
In many shapes and sizes

When it came time to pick my prize
I looked the other way
All he had to offer me was
A ribbon old and gray

Not being one to have a thought
Of graciousness and such
I felt God disappointed me
A ribbon isn't much

He understood, then vanished
As my dream became a blur
And then I thought I heard him say
We'll meet again I'm sure

The years went on and I recalled
That ribbon in my mind
As I collected blessings from
A God who was so kind

That ribbon flows through all of us
With life, with love, untold
And mine, though gray and slightly worn
Is a ribbon patched in gold

www.ingramcontent.com/pod-product-compliance
Lightning Source LLC
Chambersburg PA
CBHW041104110426
42740CB00043B/147